ESSENCE

Paintings by Alfred Ortega
Poems by Carlton Lewis Sampson

Cover art: *Bands of Colors*, oil on canvas; 48" x 36", by Alfred Ortega.
Library of Congress Catalog Number: 8908053113
ISBN: 978-1-953132-01-7 (paperback)
ISBN: 000-0-0000-0000-0 (ebook)
1. Poetry 2. Artwork
First Edition
Printed in USA

Library of Congress Catalog Number: 8025987921
ISBN: 978-0-9971140-7-2

Reprinted by permission of Carlton Lewis Sampson.

Carlton L. Sampson publisher
1311 N 26 Street
Philadlephia, Pennsylvania 19121

www.carltonlsampson.com

Contents

Preface

Alfred Ortega and I are long-time friends and mutually respected artists seeing each other occasionally over years. During a chance meeting in the fall of October 2017, Alfred Ortega suggested collaborating on a project of paintings and accompanying text commenting on the paintings. I expressed interest in the project. We updated contact information for each other and went our separate ways. In December of 2017, Alfred Ortega attended the book signing release of my graphic novel *Po Lyn Lee; Ophelia House*. We briefly discussed producing a book and agreed to work on the project sometime in the near future. Reconnecting in March of 2018, Alfred Ortega and I both took the project on in earnest in October 2018, working on the book, *Essence.*,as our primary project from November 2018 until June of 2019. Our production process followed two self-imposed rules. I did not choose the paintings, writing to what Alfred Ortega presented. Alfred Ortega did not decide on content or format of the poems. Spending over 160 hours in personal meetings and phone conversations discussing the paintings, deriving the book's title along the way, we published *Essence* in October 2019.

Introduction

In the body of *Essence,* Alfred Ortega presents paintings inspired by the dynamic between man and woman. Each poem captures Carlton Lewis Sampson's perspective on the emotional dynamics of the situation expressed in the image. Their collaboration reflects their personal bias on the essential aspect of life. Like relationships between men and women, the painting-poem paired combinations are fraught with pitfalls and laced with joy, seeking congruence as a set.

ESSENCE

Tides

Glances
Held
In
Keeping
Lost
Desire
Seeking
Eyes
See
Narcissistic
Need
To satisfy
Someone
I must
Be
Pleased
Someone
Objectified
Ripples
Their
Opposing
Beach

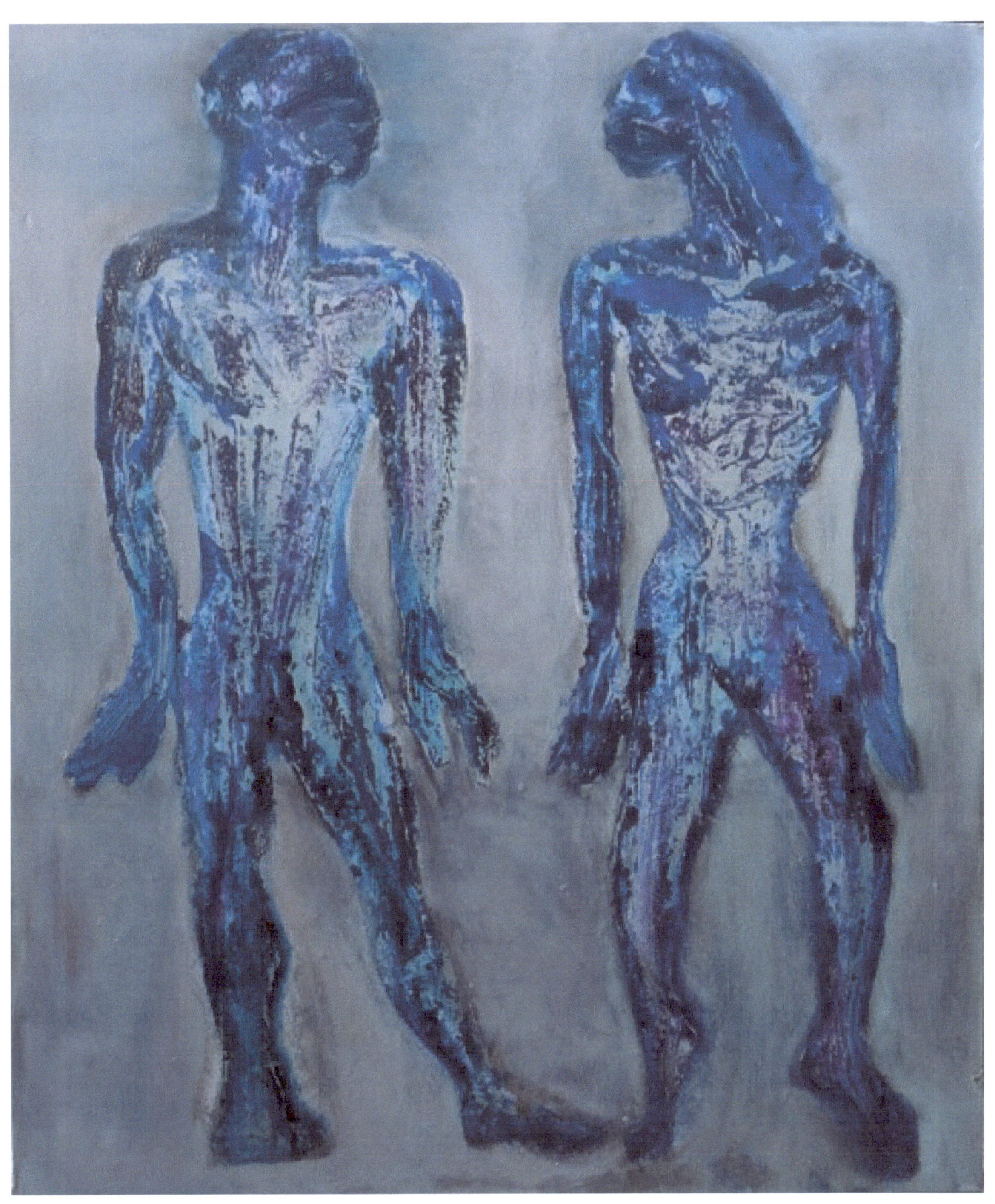

The Very Beginning

Quiver

Sat Cupid
High in a willow
Demon eyed
On his next prize
Two people
In a meadow
Lying
Side by side.

Cupid's job
Was simple
Spread humanity
Here and about
And if in hearts
It flourished
The species would
Not die out.

It mattered not
To Cupid
His job
Shoot hearts
True
An eternity
Of arrows
Dwindled down
To just two.

Two arrows
In Cupid's quiver
Argued
As demon arrows do
Debating the arrow
Cupid delivered
The heart
Cupid shoots thru.

Stood Cupid
High on a branch
In the willow tree
Taking two arrows in his fists
Breaking them over his knee
And as the arrows gasped
Cupid
Shouted,
Cupid
Laughed,
"God!
To hell with humanity
You can't make Love
From bad shafts."

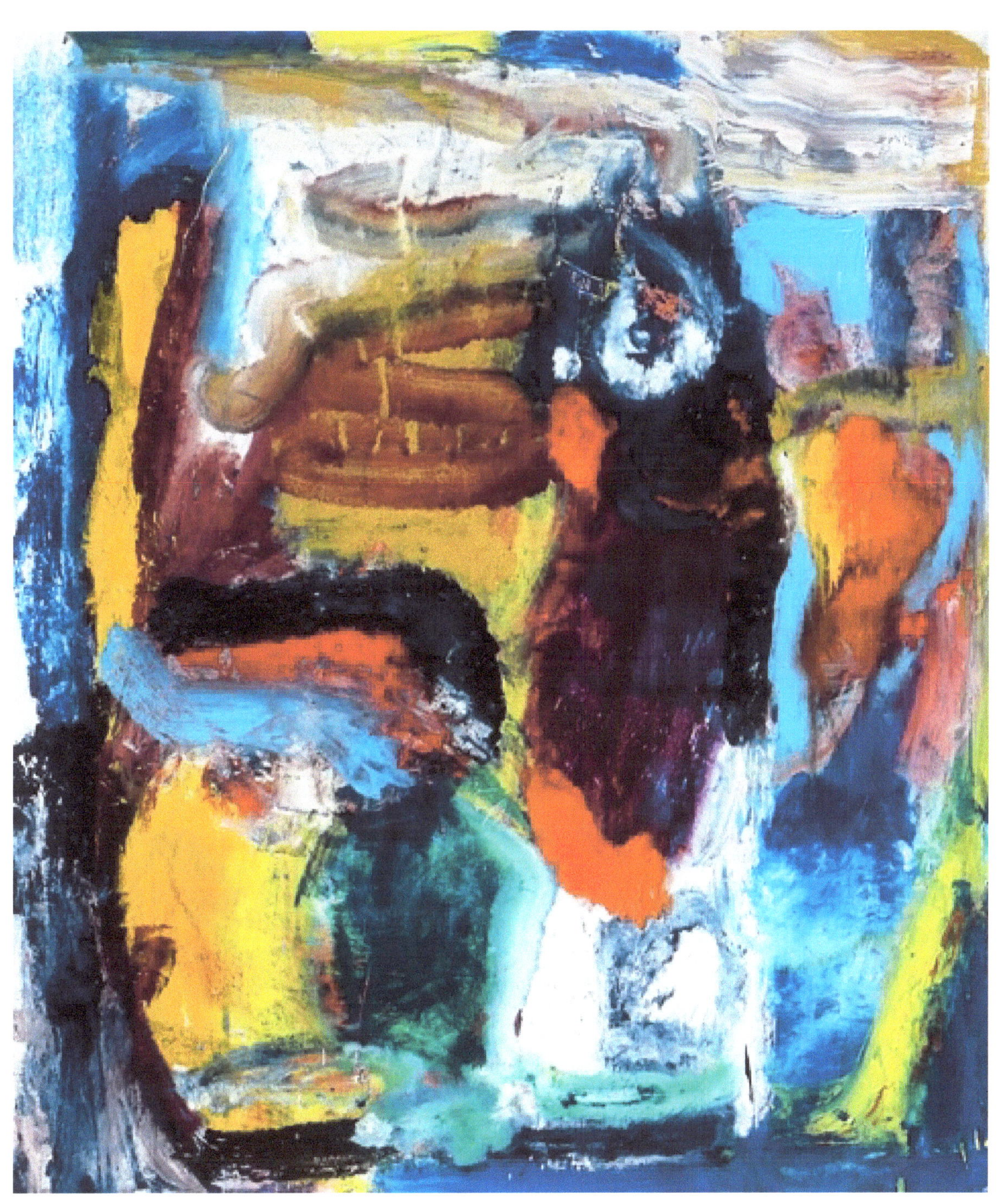

The Search for Sophocles

Muse

She sits
With her
Man
And smiles
Why are you alone?
How much do you want?
How willing are you to give?
Come I'll
Please you
It's my pleasure
All my own
No one can take it
From me
No one can give me
What I want
No one is my
Need
Come
And you
Will see
In her eyes
On her face
Oneliness
Her essence
An alluring
Breeze
Blows
Hearts away
Like tumbleweeds
Rolling
Chased
Pleasant
Memories
While
She sits
With her
Man
And smiles

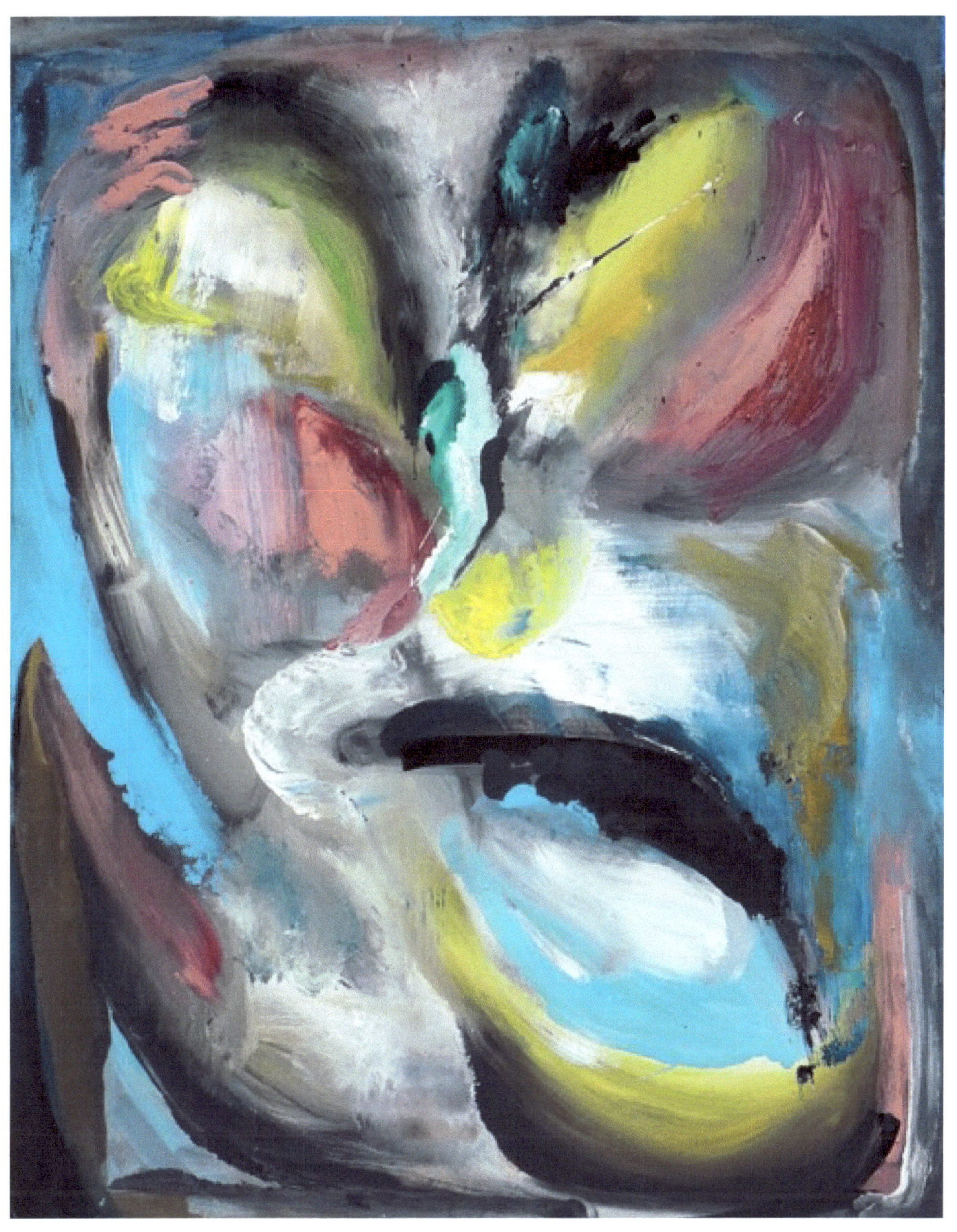

She Is There

Twixt

Flesh
Wanting
Need
Filled
Yearning
Obsessed
Driven
Anxiously
Feeling
Fulfillment
Nourishing
Replenishment
Complete
Separate
Touch
Reaching
Caressing
Up
Over
Across
Thru
Space
Down
Between

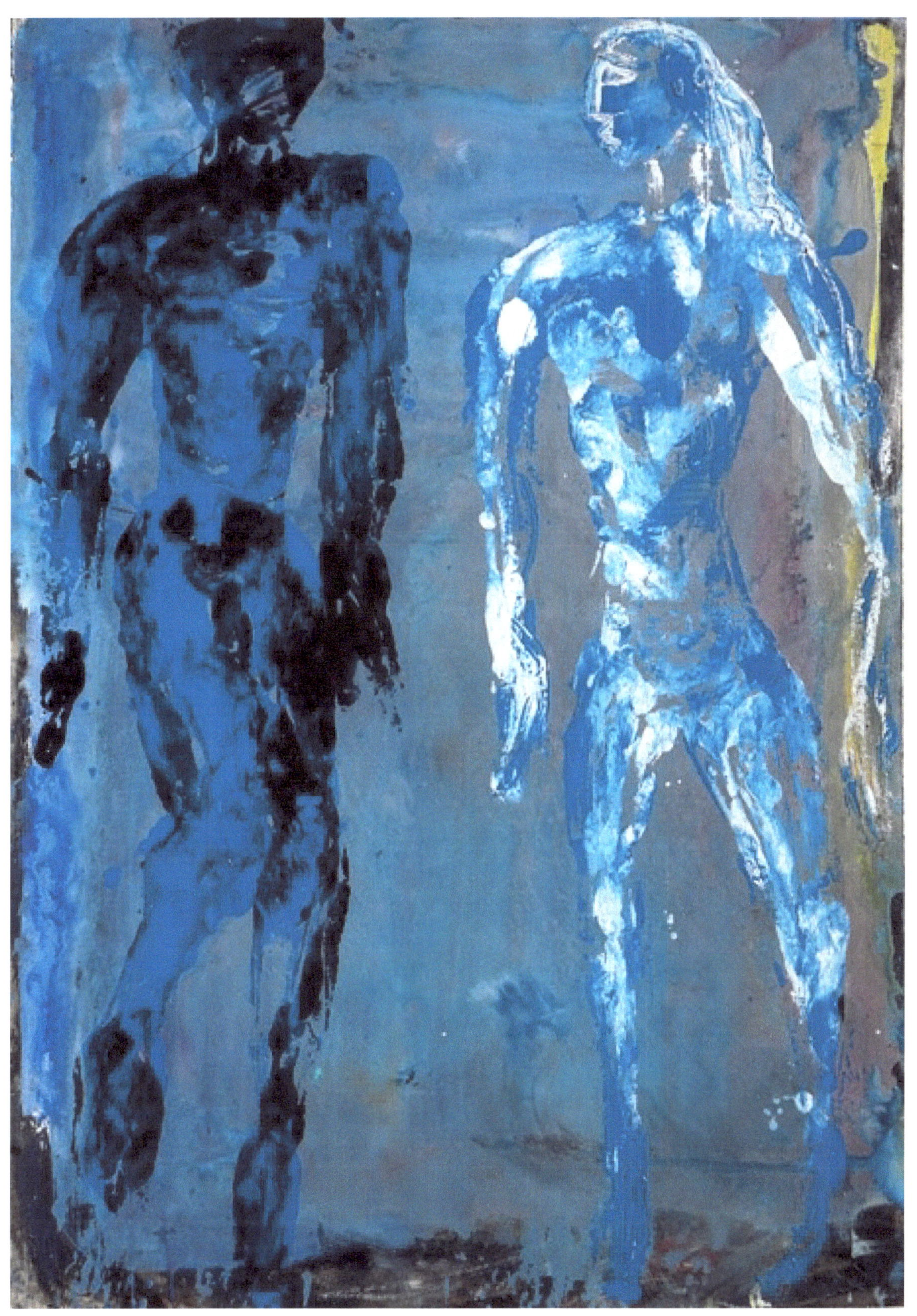

A MAN and A WOMAN

Plumage

Riding
High
Cocky
Dancing away
Inviting
In Joey
She sees
Happiness
Caring
Courageousness
Strength
Kindness
Holds her
Satisfying
Her
Needs
She experiences
Ecstasy
On demand
Caged
Tied
To his
World

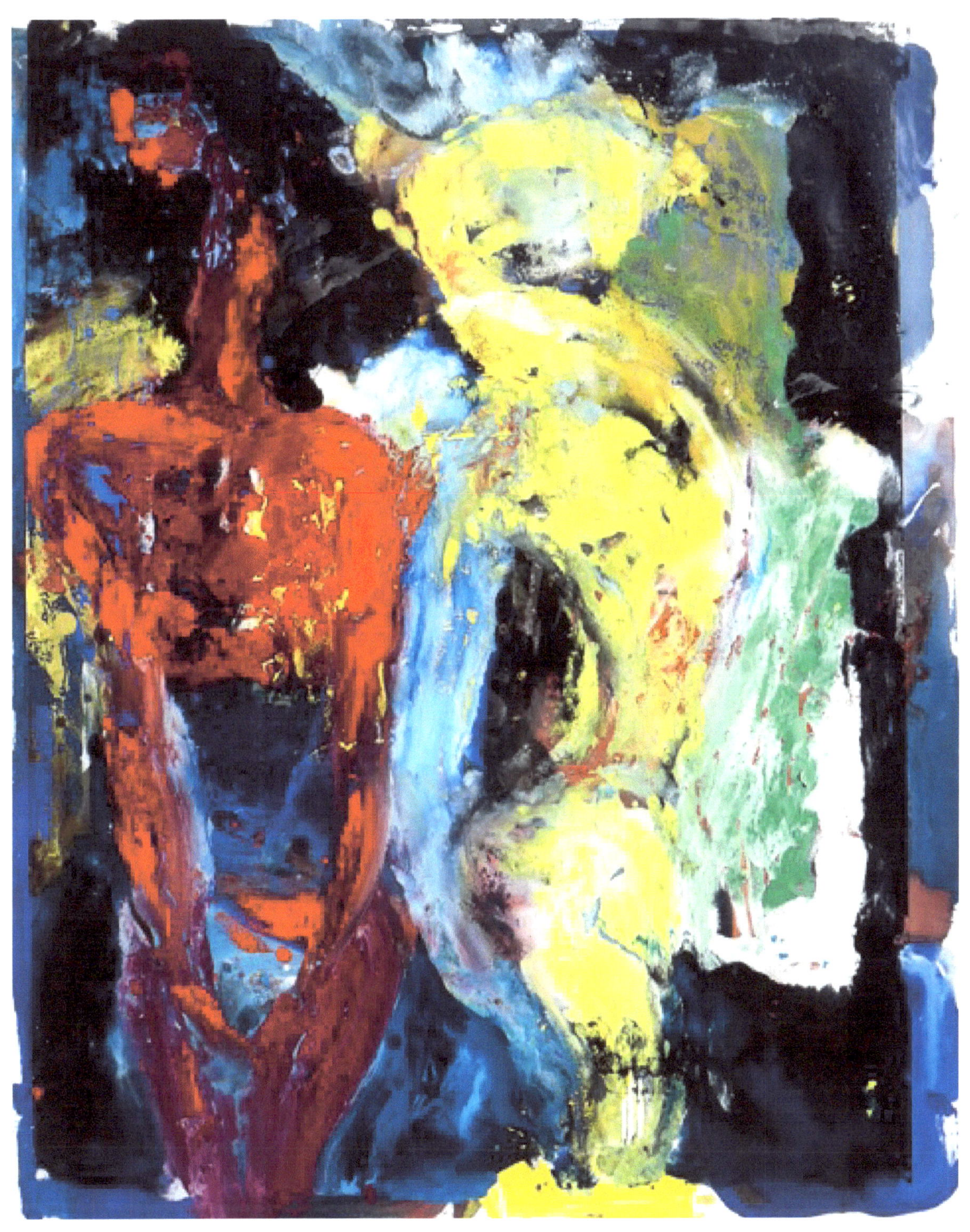

Better Get Into You

Sensuous Kiss

At the edge
Down a crevasse
Under a bright
Sunny sky
She dances
Holding a torch
Beating
A fire drum
He stands
Pulling toward her
With force

She flees
Her hair
Braided flame
Floating behind
He hides
Head masked
Save the eyes

A child at his chest
And butler
Aide
Operating
His ass licking
Machine
Riding below
Like a dog
His real face
Is seen
Her curvaceousness
His sought nose
Over
River
Valley
Mountains
She leaps
Tiptoe

Cross meadows
Above cliffs
Shimmering lake
Waterfalls
Flow

Beyond
The deep
Dark wood
In Cupid's
Hollow
I saw
Spirits
Romance

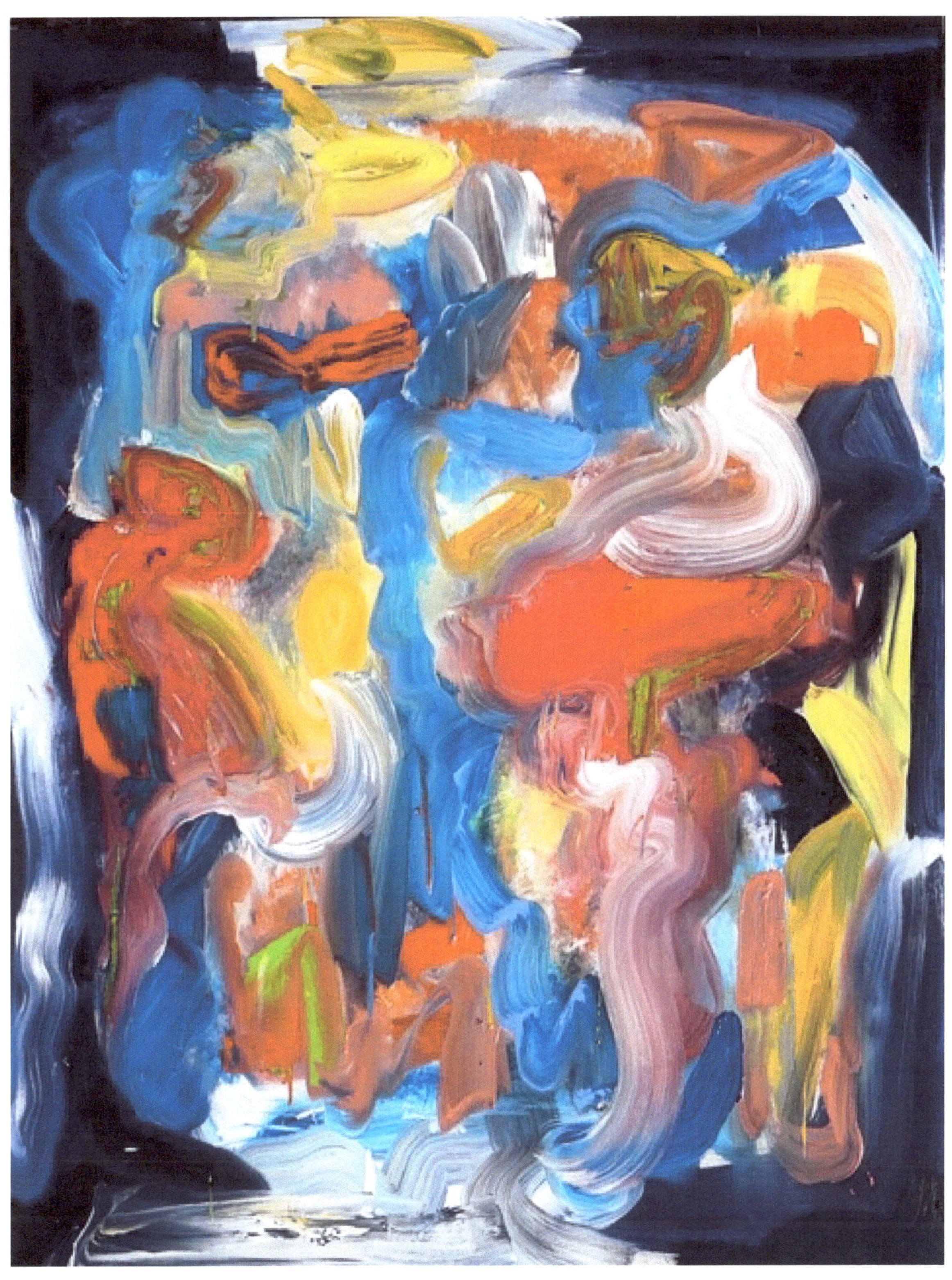

The Empty Sail Takes the Wind

The Gift

Received
Unwanted
Elating
Act
Ecstatic
Actions
Carry
Desire
Growing
Satisfaction
Happiness
Achieved
Giving

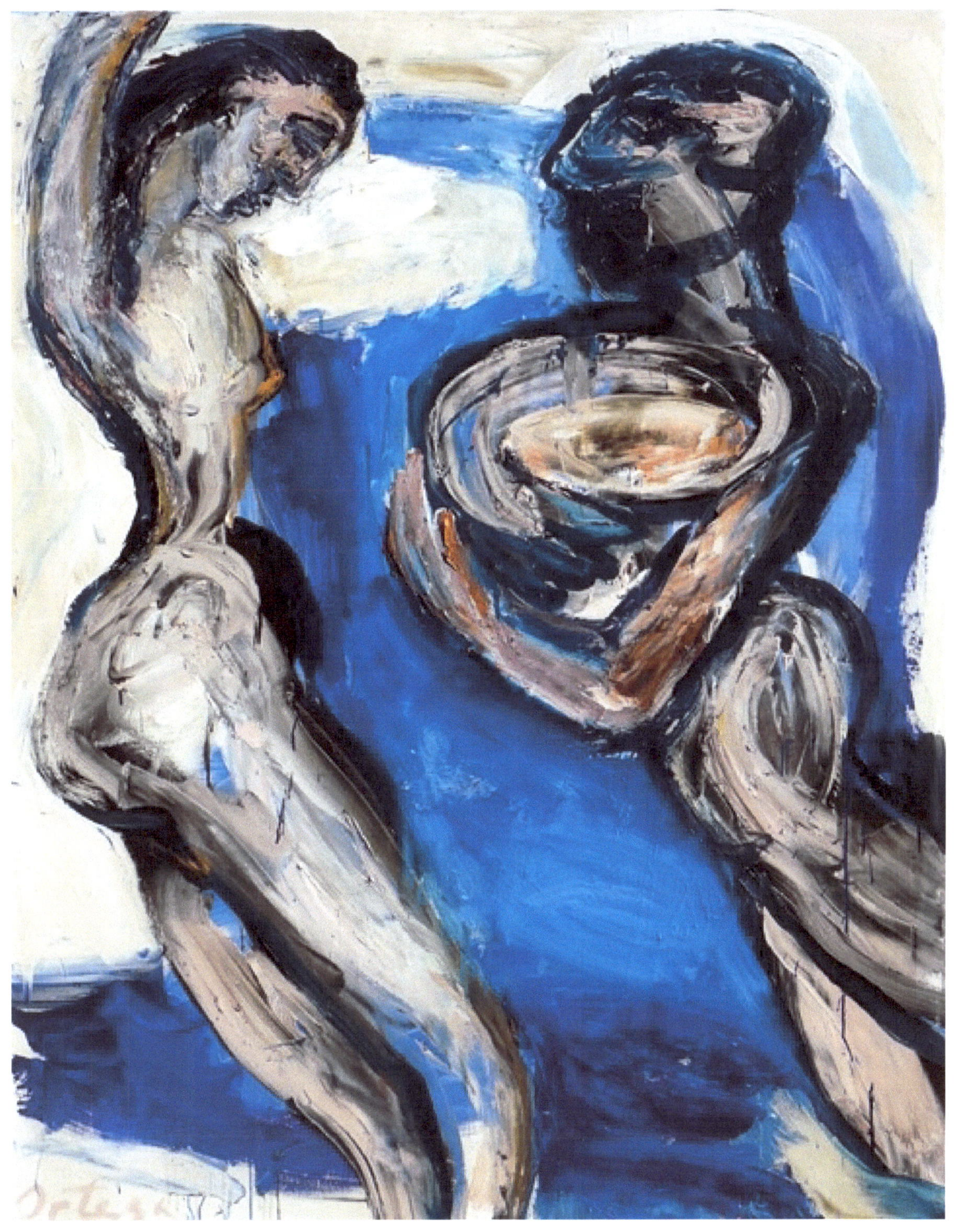

The Gift

Others

Like
Bright
Light
Streaks
Piercing
Plane
Apertures
Growing
Into
Darkness
Filling
Flesh
Feeling
Space
Around
Bodily
Moment
Experience
Within
Action
Resulting
Now
Known
Then
Akin
Flesh
Bound
Present
Presence

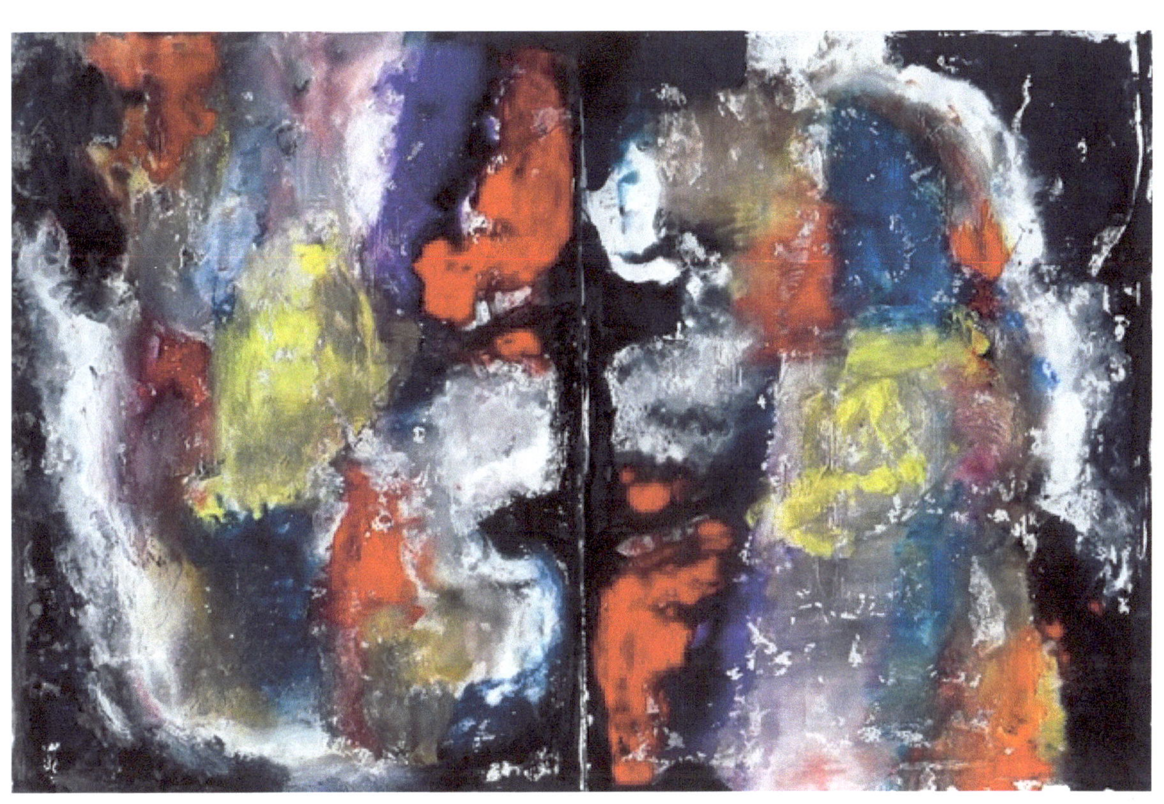

Which One is the Mask

Shout

No words
Speechless
Trust
Dissolved
Broken
Promise
Failed
Embrace
Refused
Forgiveness
Virtueless
Dismissed
Disregarded
Challenged
Truths

Selfless
Fingertips
Cover
His
Lips
Disappointment
Echoes
Her
Sighs
Disheartened
Dissatisfied
Seeking
Himself
She
Glances
Goodbye
Leaving
Him
Exposed
Hollow
Inside

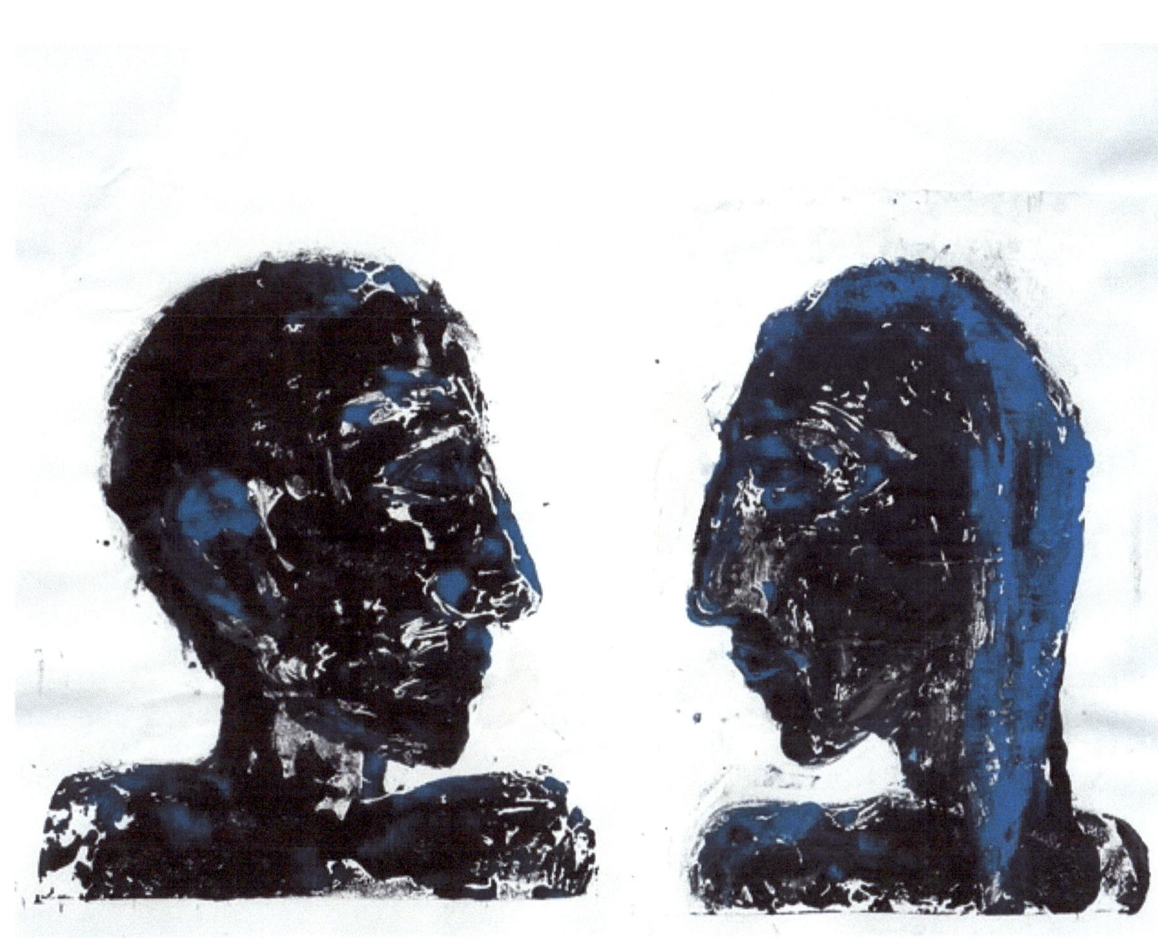

A Man and a Woman on White

Choice

Illuminating
Her
He
Comes
On
Strong
Contending
Everything
For
Her
Touch
Promise
Beyond
Belief
Truthful
Certain
Stance
Nothing
Accepted
Nothing
Refused
Her
Toes
Readily
Dance
Innately
Yearning
He is
A seed
She wants
To grow
She
Must
Decide

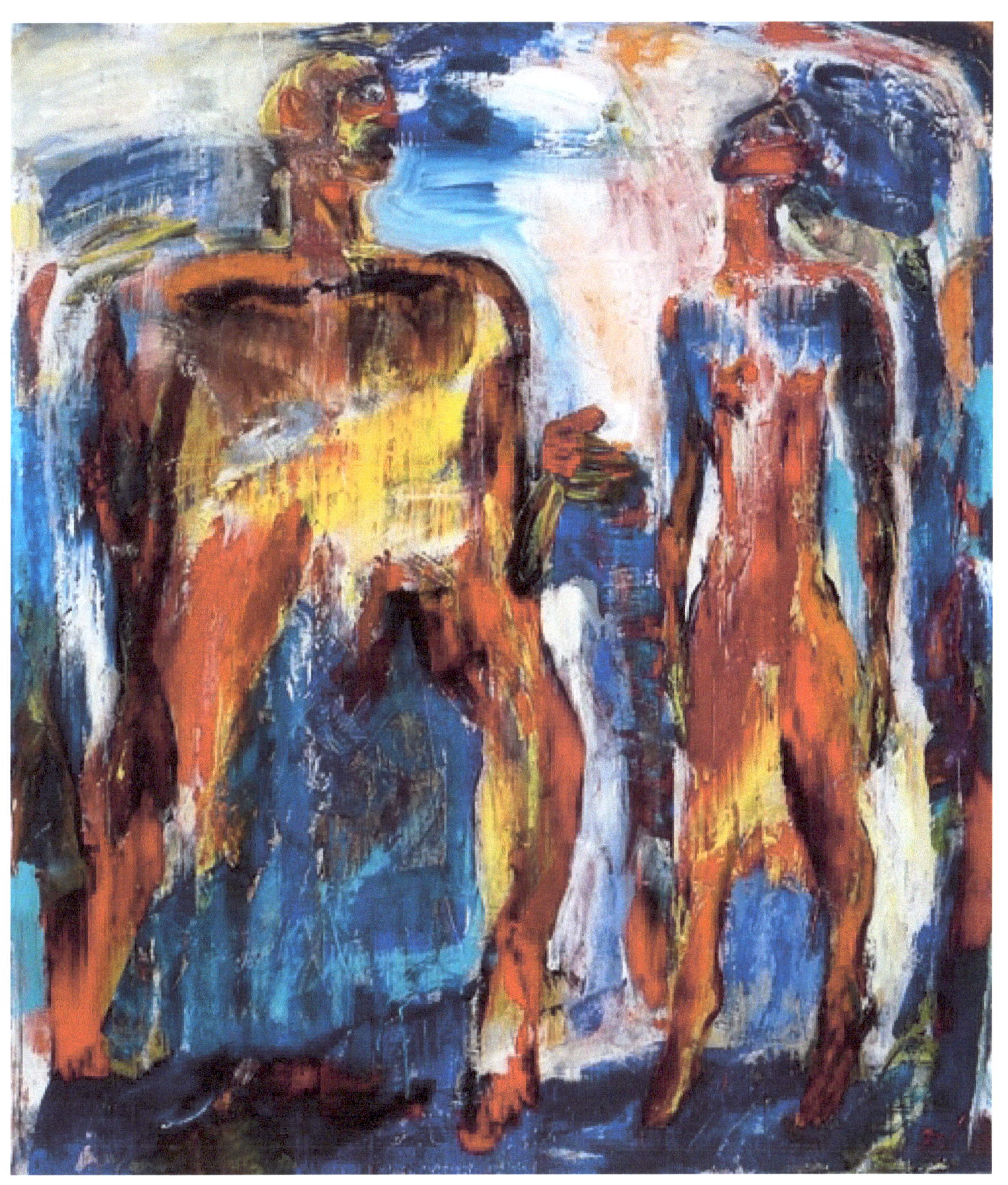

The Offering

The Infinity Dance

The Firestorm twins
Went out to dance
Properly helmeted
Shielded from glance

Driven by Chance
An unregistered star
From their cool blue cave
To the Burning Hut Bar

At the Burning Hut Bar
The show forever begins
On a floor in man's head
Under a ball that spins

Blow by Burning Hut Bar
Aura's top listed thing to do
Blowing in past Horizon
Aura spied the Firestorm crew

"Hmm twin firestorms
A hot helmeted pair."
The Firestorms grew heated
As Aura glared

"The glaring aura
Foolish, un-cool."
"Time we teach
The aura rules."

The Firestorms blazed
Moving Aura's way
When echoed the Horizons,
"Let infinity play!"

Fuming the twins flared
Aura burst to arrays
Engulfing the Firestorms
Billowed a philter haze*

The Firestorm Aura infinity
Is physical is lewd
Allured other dancers joined
Infinite erotic moves

"Stop the music," echoed the Horizons
Working the Burning Hut Bar
"You crossed a line
Way beyond too far!

"Get a motel room
Go do it in a bed
Stop infinity dancing
On this floor in man's head!"

Sparked a Firestorm,
"What you spin is allowed!"
"No philters," echoed the Horizons,
"Look at the crowd!

"Put on your helmet
Your dance is done
You, Aura, your twin
Equals infinity plus one!

"Take it outside, Aura,
And take your Firestorm friends,"
Echoed the Horizons
Under a ball that spins

The Firestorm twins smoldered
As Aura got off the floor
All Burning Hut Horizons
Showed dancers the door

So the Firestorm twins and Aura
Chanced-it
To Club Physical Space
To infinity dance uncounted
In Horizon's new place.

*Philter; a potion, charm, or drug that causes arousal and sexual passion.

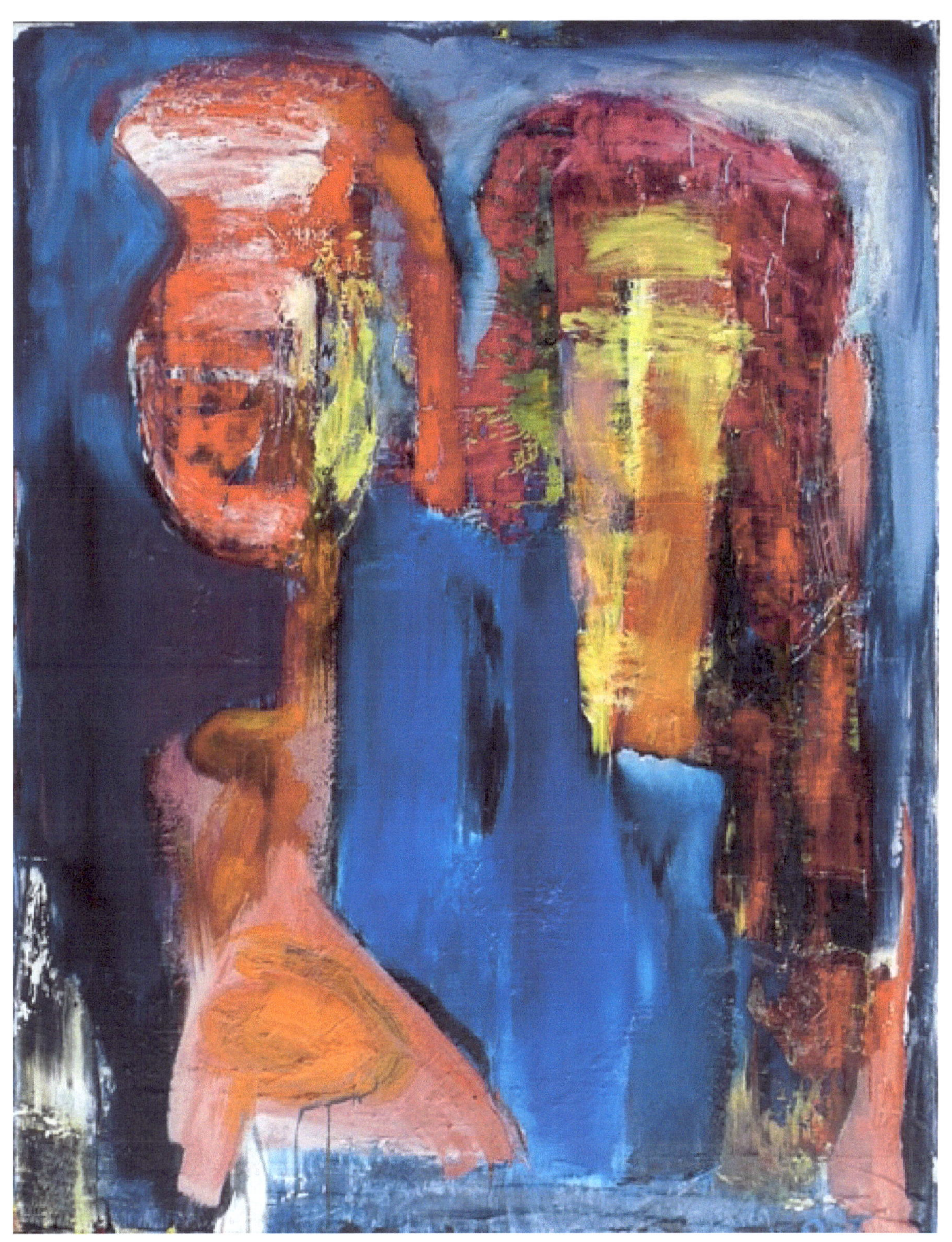

The Woman with Red Hair

Fair Exchange

Zero
Feeling
Nothing
Touched
Apprised
Situations
Dialogue
Remembered
Accurately
Foretold
Leaving
Seeking
Approaching
Facing
Another
Reaching
Outwardly
Glowing
Shared
Embrace
Stone
Cold
Hard
Inside
Beguiling
Walking
Hurt
Walking
Pain
Moving
On
Fair
Exchange

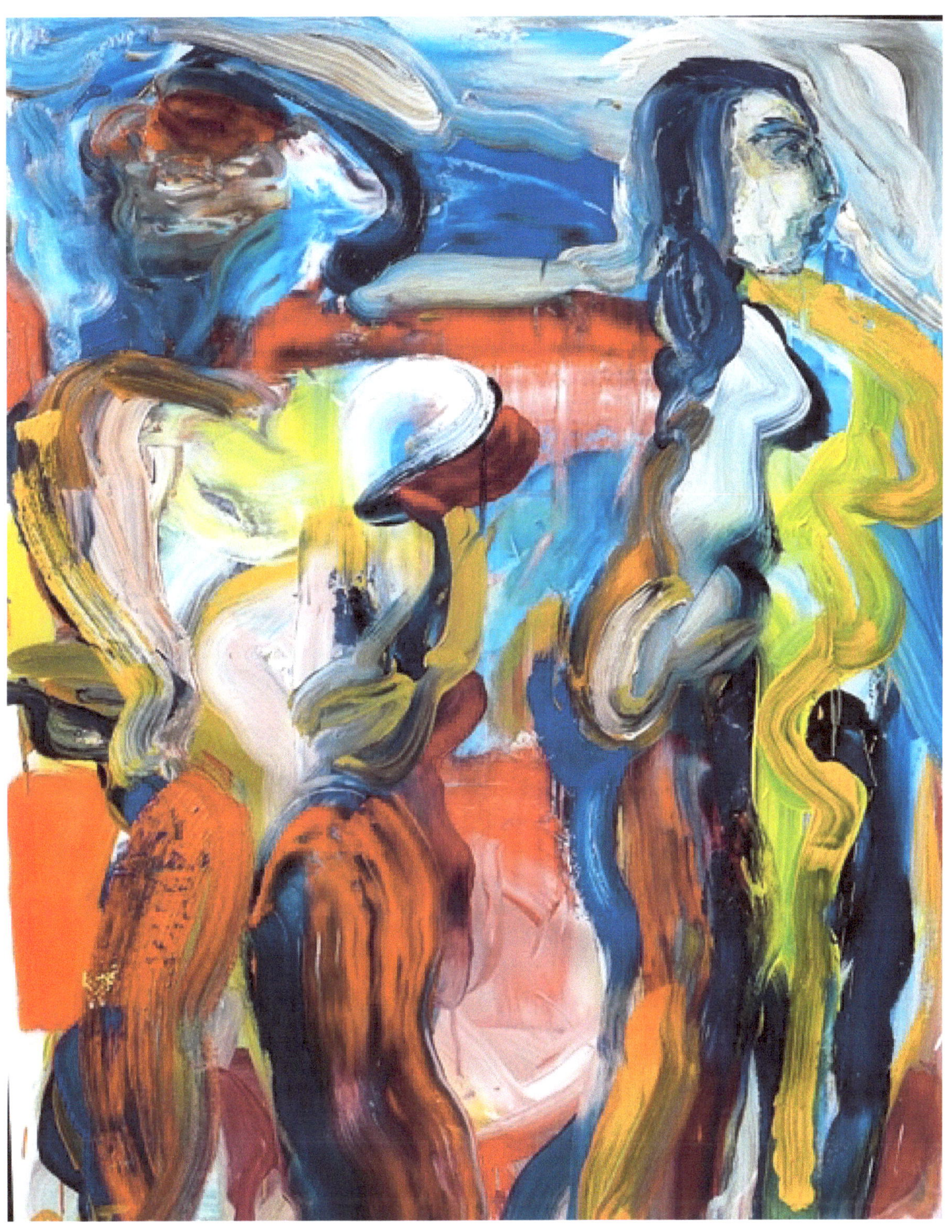

Heart In the Box

Gladiator

Standing heart shielded
Kept deep within
His protected treasure
Never exposed again

He refuses running
Discounting happenstance
Seeking a certain someone
A certain type romance

Out fielding encounter
His narrow vision's stance
Has gravity to its attraction
Alluring women by glance

Luscious lipped greetings
Returned flirtatious hints
Glanced heart shielding
Time without her spent

Salacious tempting overtures
Nights of delight implied
Standard response refrain
Shielded heart denied

His gaze graciously avoided
His protected deep insides
Suddenly brought to surface
By reflecting compassionate eye

She comes intent smiling
Into his depth she stares
Wondering, whispering her parley,
"I'll treasure this please share."

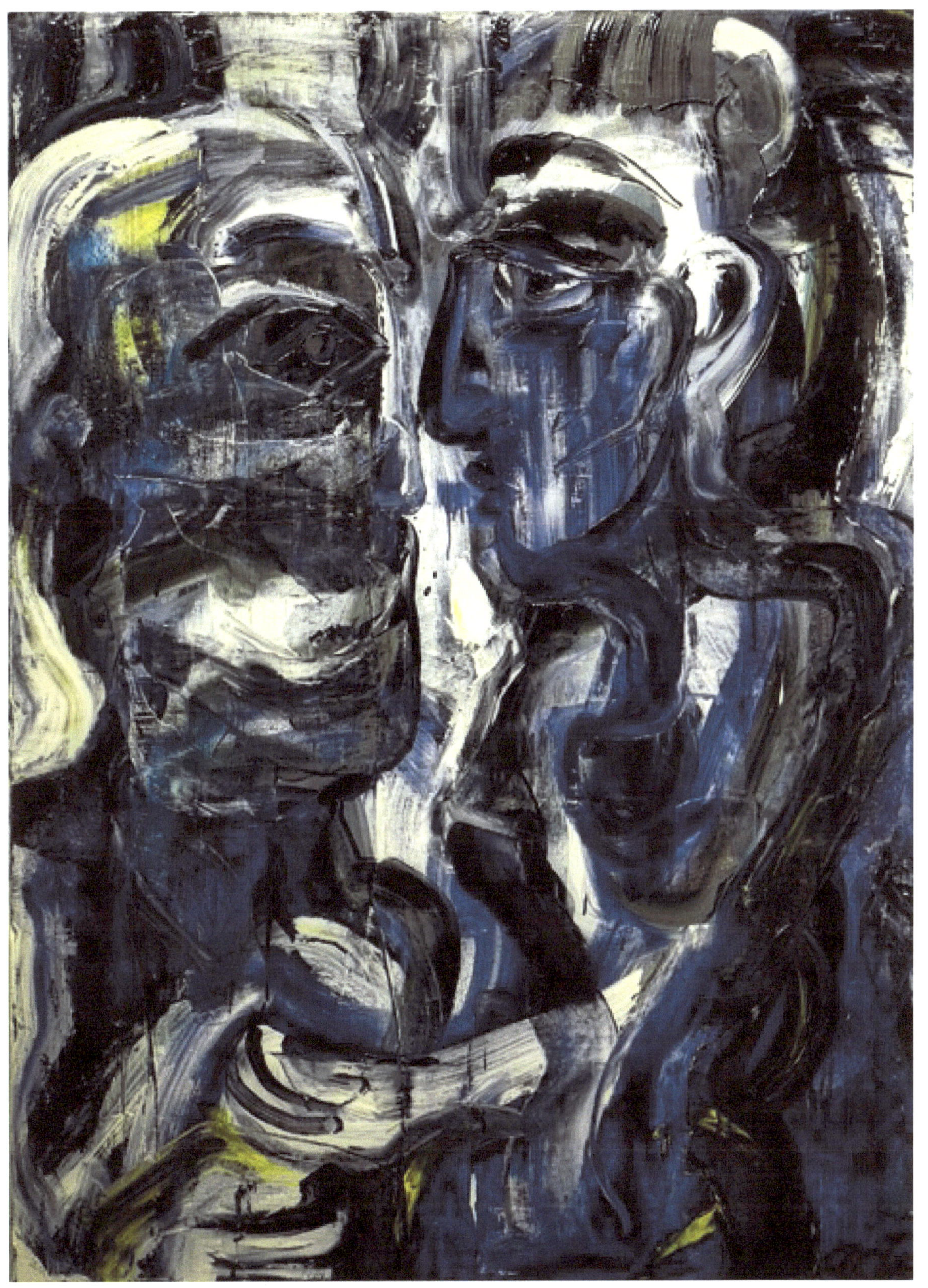

The Two Lovers

Chemistry

Triumphantly he walks
Idolizing fixed belief
Fended fears crushed
Petals at his feet

She trusting openly seeking
Satisfying her needs
He defenseless culprit
In her pains to be

Pulled together yearning
Prodding for embrace
Wanting, waiting, wondering
Tantalizing his space

Present anxiously longing
Being with her again
His nerves spark aligning
Pleasured beneath her skin

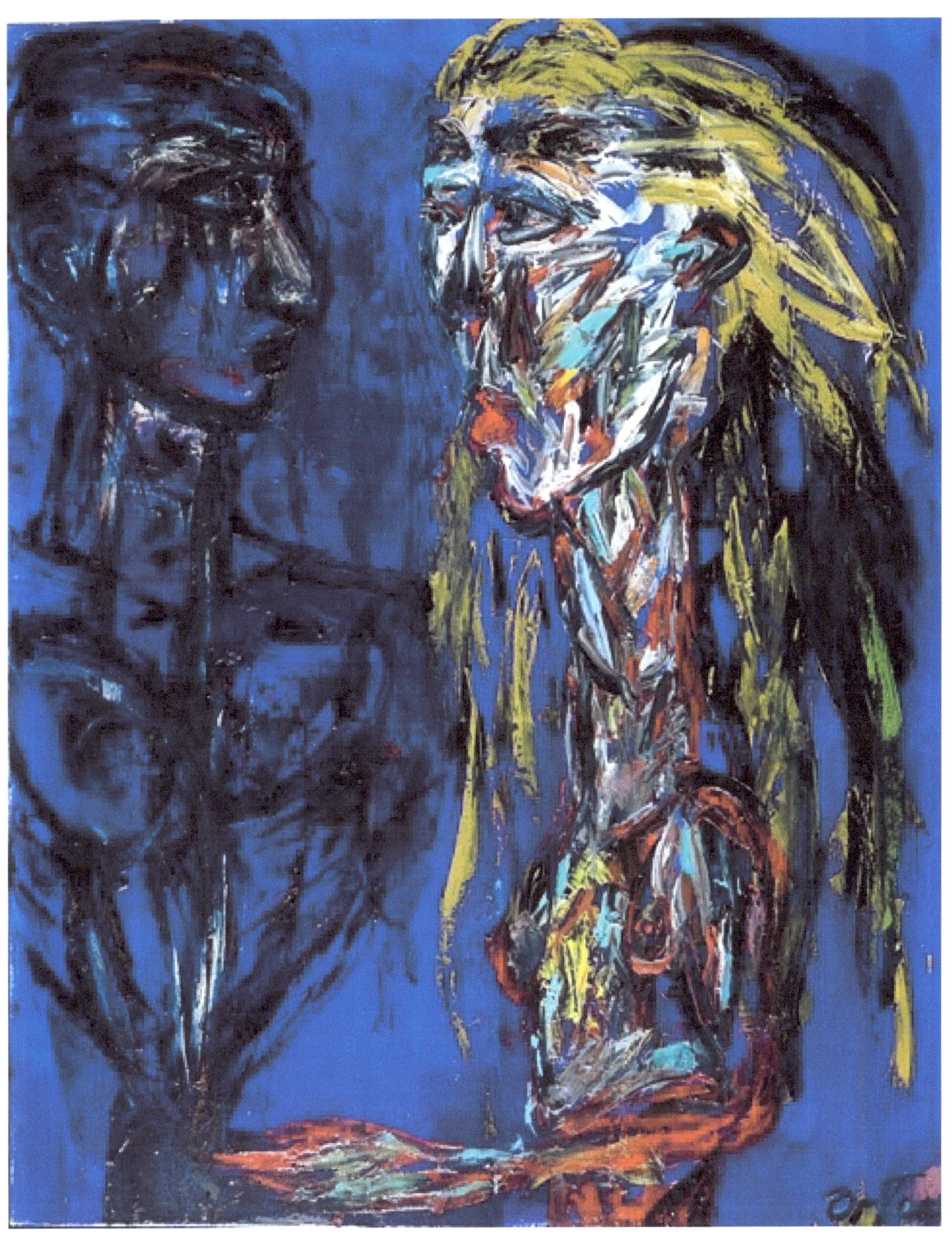

Sacristy / Shattered

Breach

She walks into silence
Catching every eye
Melissa is a presence
Someone who arrives

Sometimes she listens
Sometimes she cries
She comes seeking me
My support my advice

People of means with offerings
Resourcefully for Melissa vie
Proposing promising friendships
Tenderness a prize

Taking for satisfaction
Giving needs alone
Partners serving purpose
Someone their own

Holding on clinging
Failing to recognize
Discovering Melissa
Failure to realize

Experiencing Melissa
Within intimacy immersed
Feeling for pleasure
Satisfying a thirst

Ecstasy unfulfilled
Melissa openly shares
Passionate meaningless memories
Longing to be there

"Be with me Melissa."
My thoughts give me away
In her eyes my answer
Melissa's silent, "..."

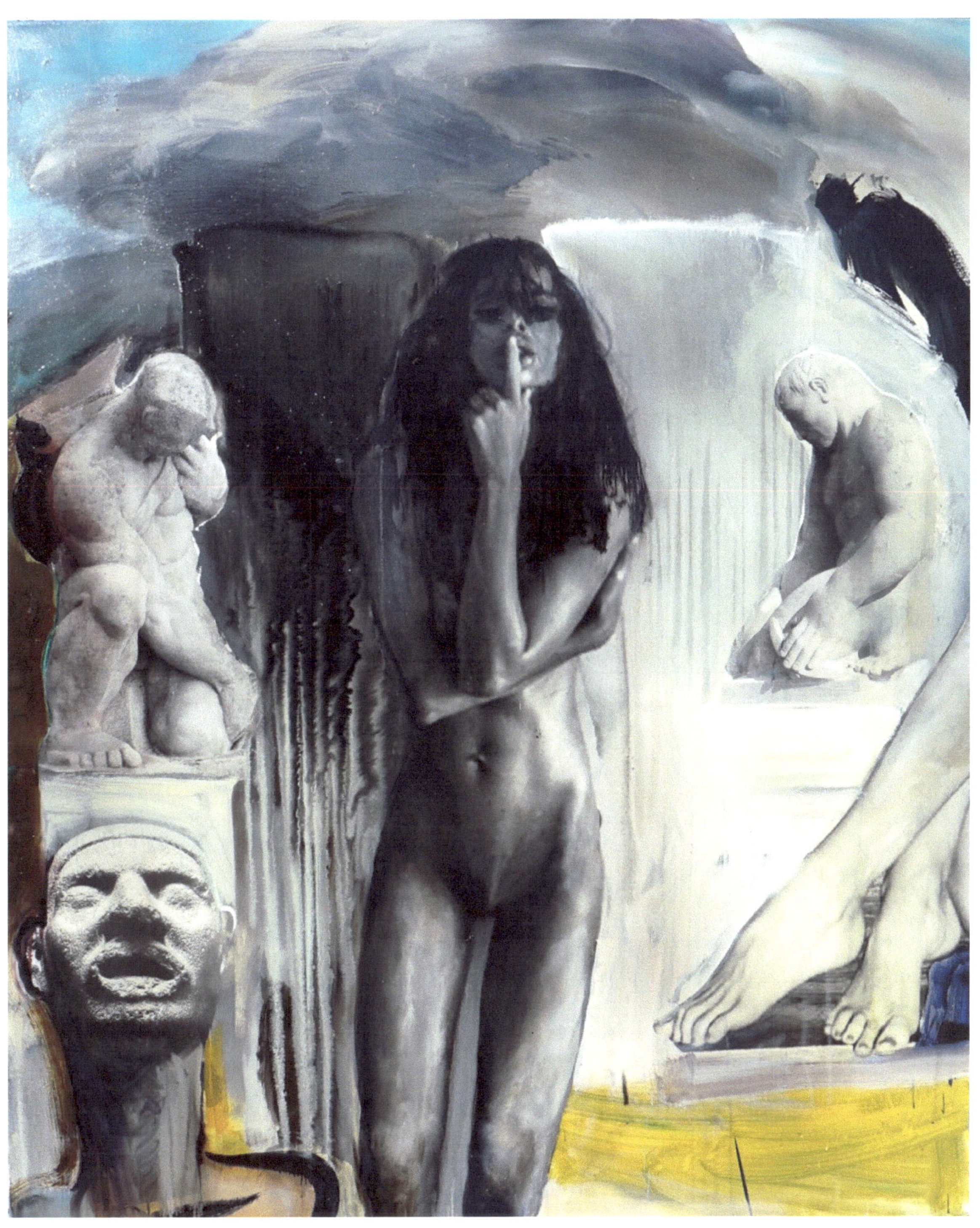

Stormy Sunshine

Eden

Torn
Nurtured
Forced
Pulled
Impacting
Bodies
Ecstasy
Engendered
There
Now
Content
Fulfilled
Grateful
Present
Aware
Predisposed
Accepting
Expecting
Anticipating
Totality
Moment
Together
Flesh
Shared
Feeding
Growing
Days
Light
Joining
Producing
Tomorrows
Torn

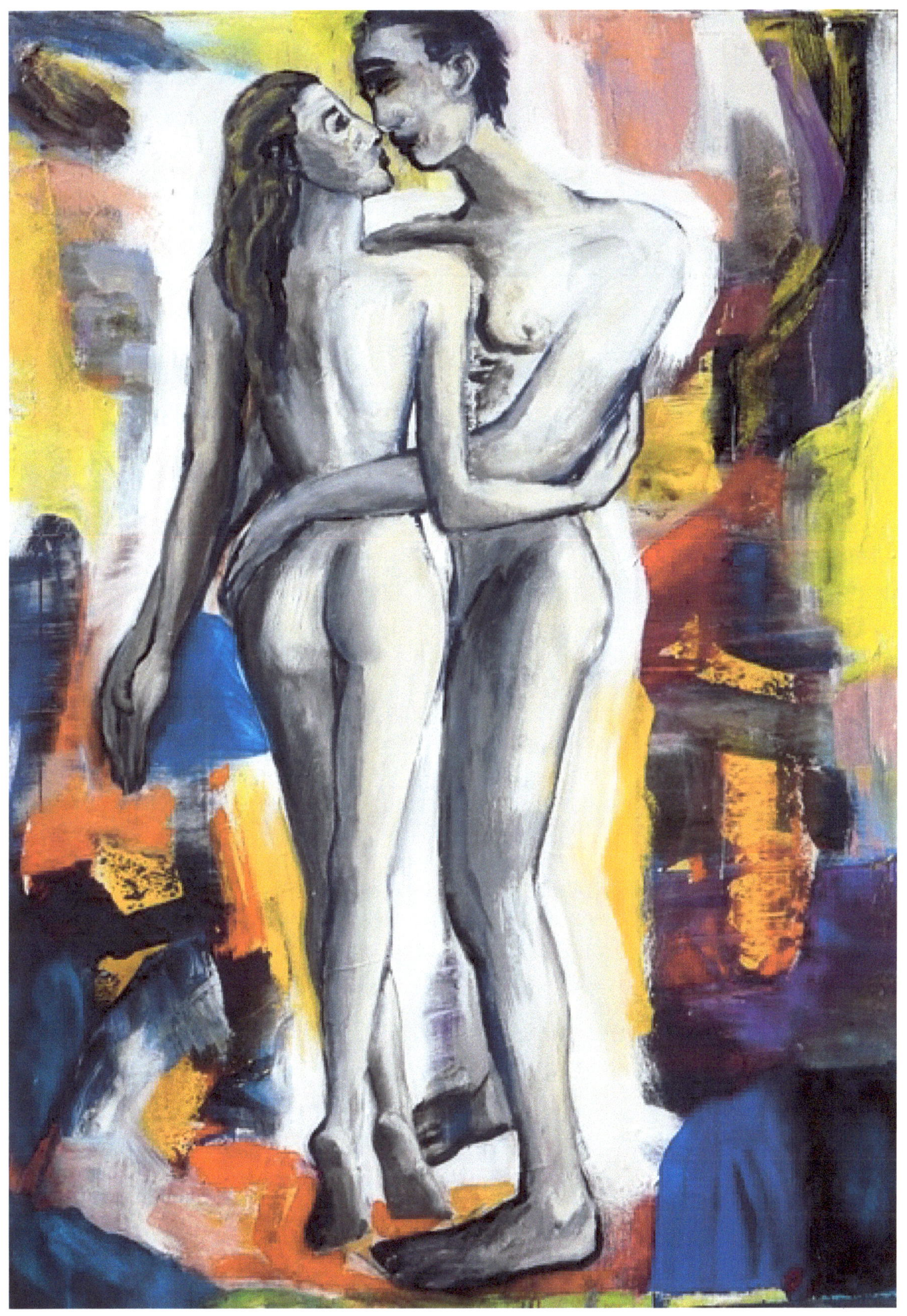

Presence

There

Too close for conversation
Save between their eyes
Given chance taken
Platonic past aside

Accepted silent invitation
From someone who always cared
Moment of realization
Unspoken adoration shared

Succumbing to mutual attraction
A friendship's promise breached
For long sought fulfillment
True intimacy within reach

Everything learned released let go
Knowing who they'll find
Trusting in each other
Together there in mind

Immersing interaction
Emotions passionately conveyed
Pulling in particular fashion
Guiding a certain sway

Against a wall supporting
Two impacting bodies collide
Experiencing union
Feeling held deep inside

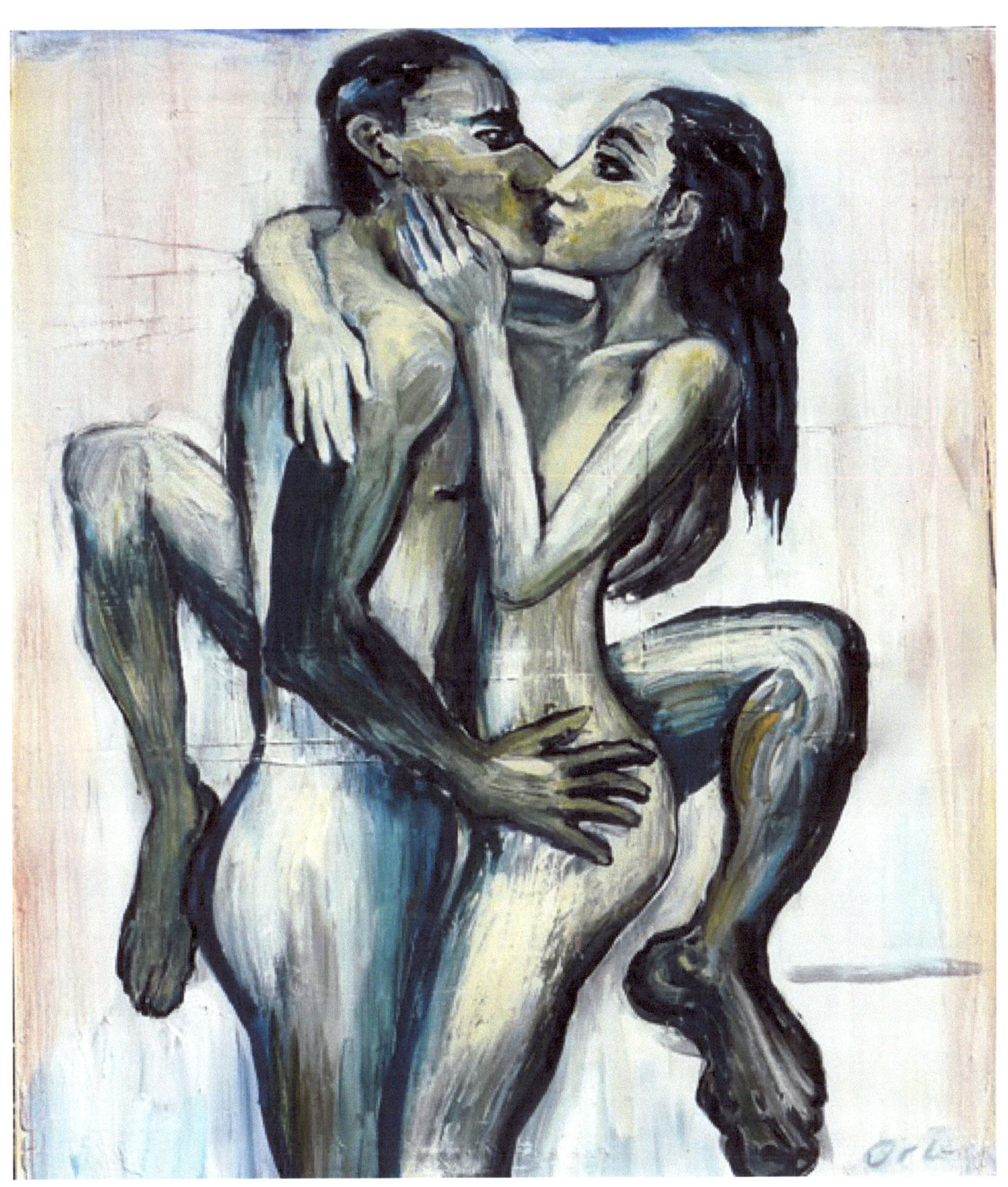

Standing in the Promised Land

Cornerstone

She comes to him wanting
His desire for her to be pleased
His dominion provides
Her submissive intent shielding
Veiled by his presence
She satisfies both
With his strength
She finds time
Defended

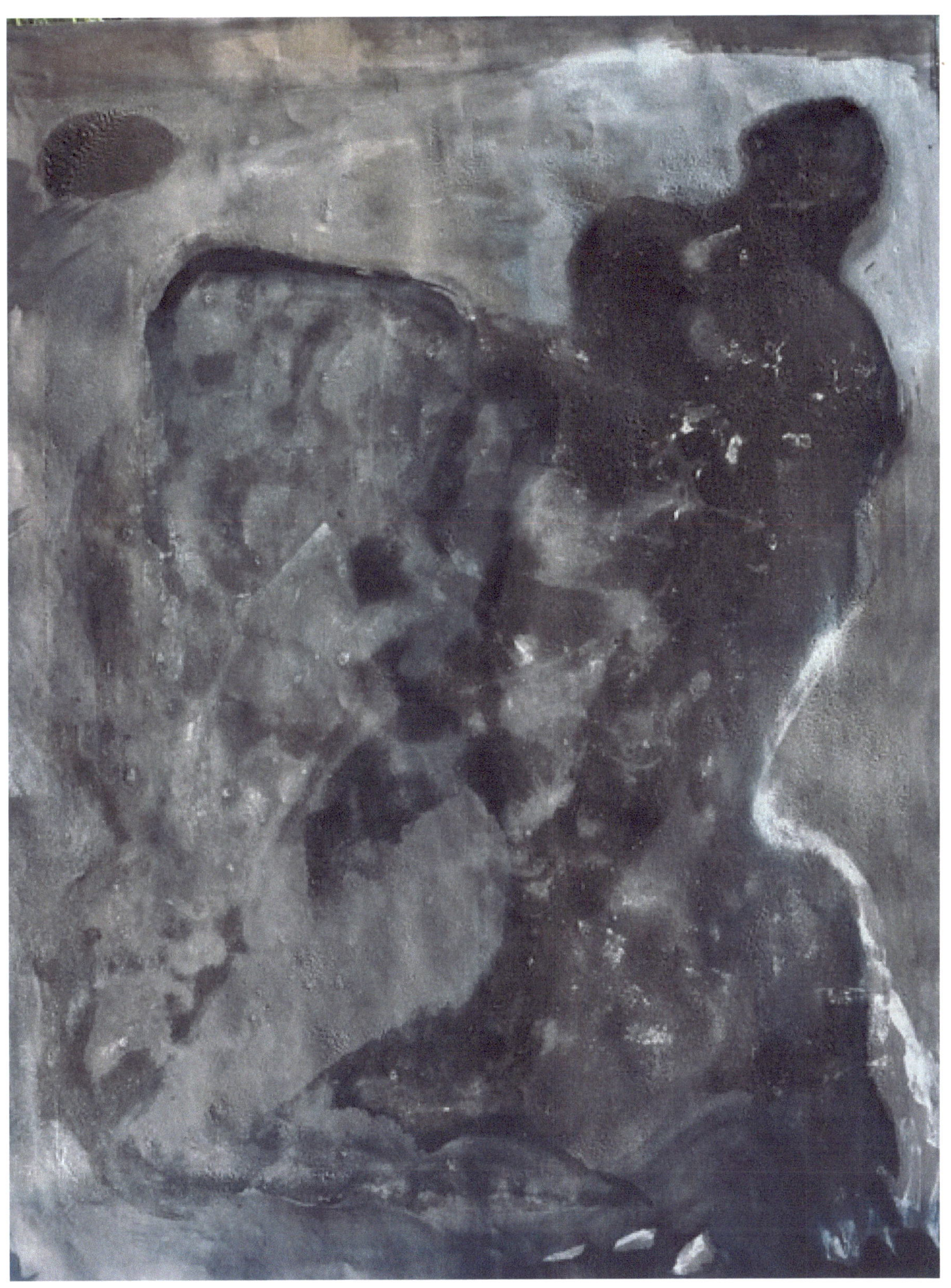

Shades of Love

Us

Tomorrow
Still
Together
Like
Yesterday
Breathless
Last
Night
Between
Kisses
Gasping
Air
Left
Wet
Dangling
Need
Holding
Passed
Out
Sweaty
Sticky
Moist
Embracing
Morning
Comes
Satisfying
Fulfilling
Beginning
New
Days
Moments
Granted
Touching
Us

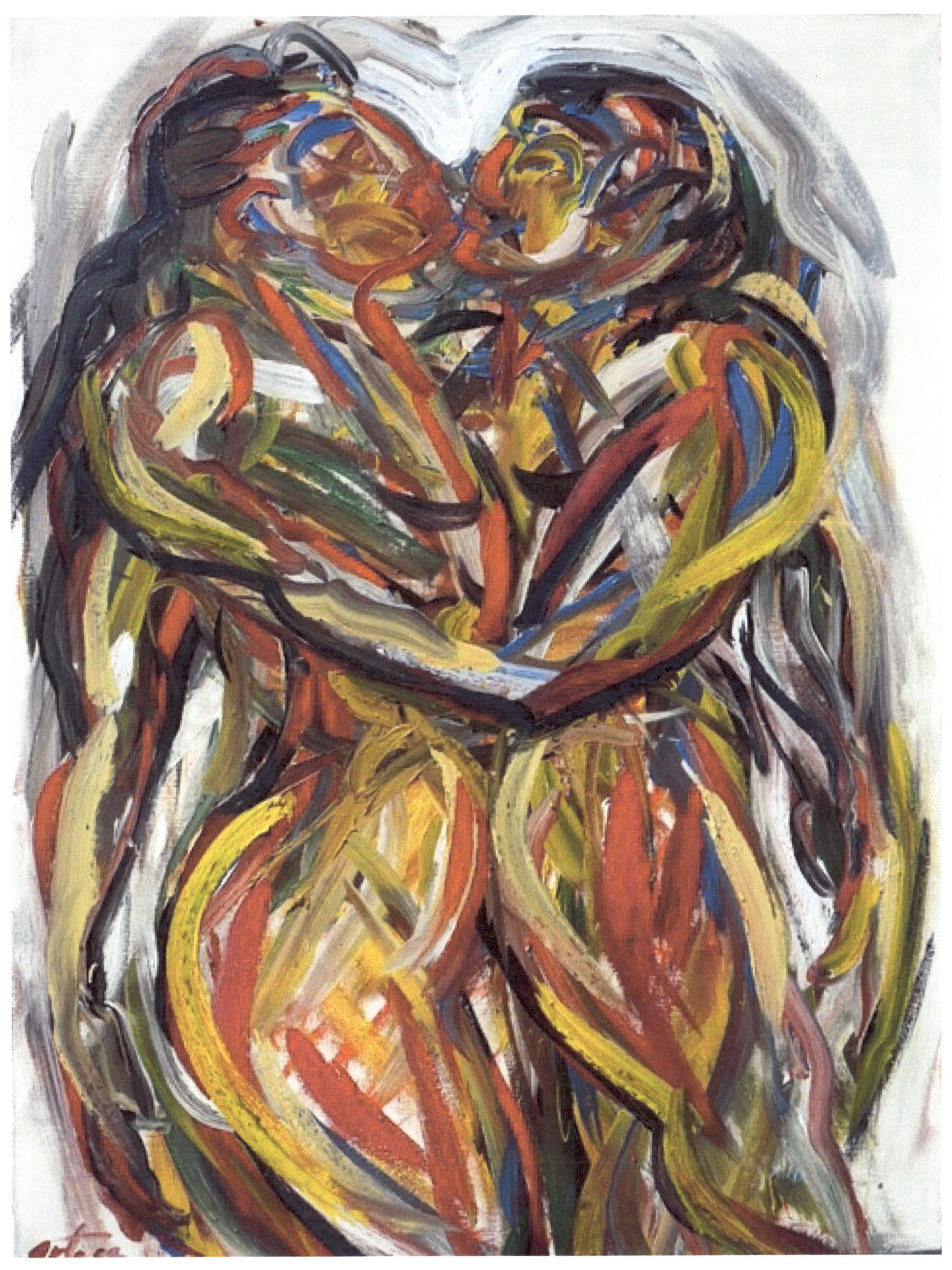

The Lovers

'...Okay.'

She just knows he just knows
Give getting needs satisfied
Both pursuing their pleasure
Wanting each other inside

Hours spent embracing
Smiling laughing just because
Wondrous anticipation awaiting
Wondering what another does

In ten, twenty years, and now
Walking while holding hands
At sixty, seventy, eighty-five
Bare feet scrunch beach sand

Tickling
Giving
Hearts
Sharing
Bodies
Seeing
Eye
To
Eye
Joined
Mine
Enjoying
Their
Other
As is
Sexy
Together
Alive

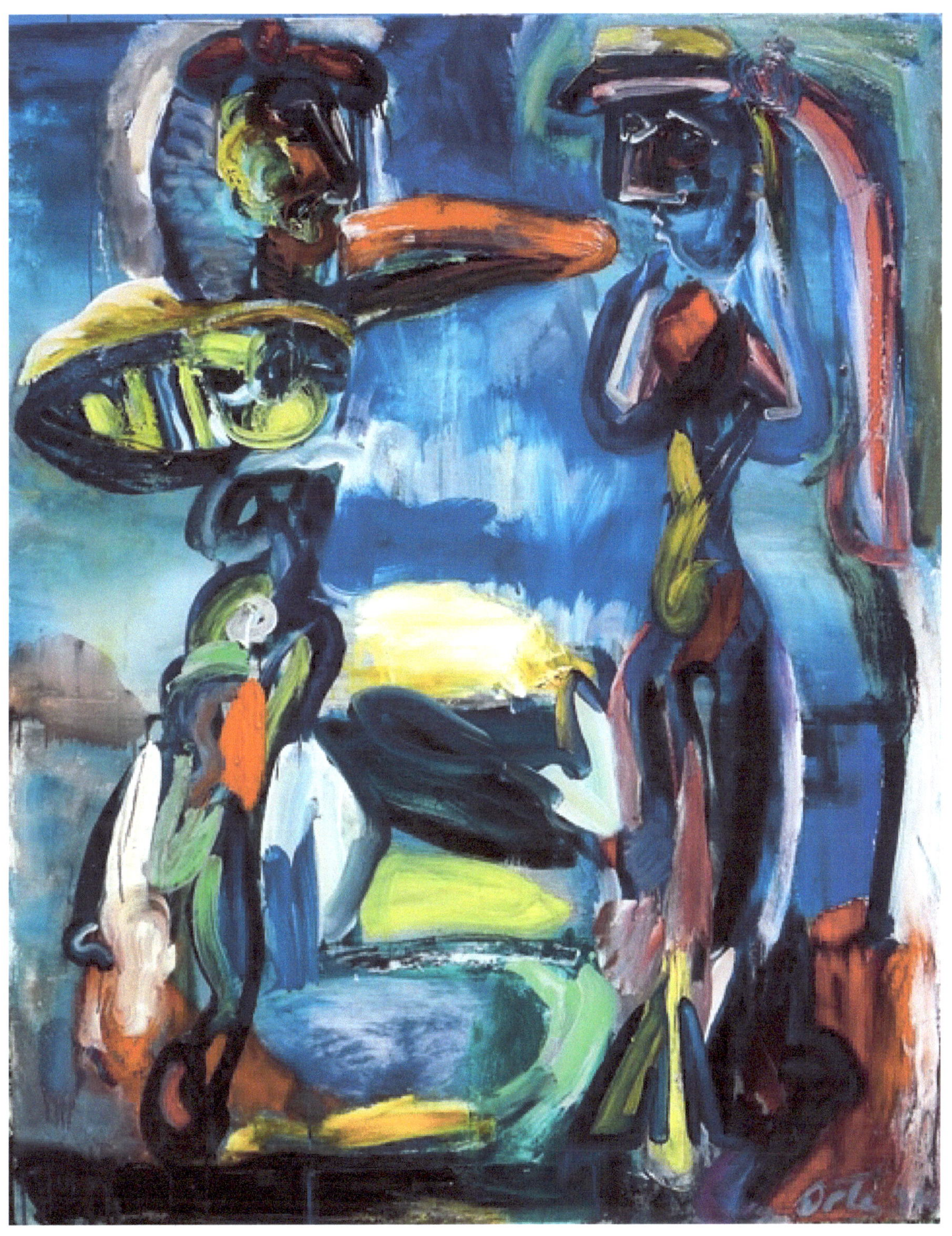

Summer Madness

List of plates

About the Author

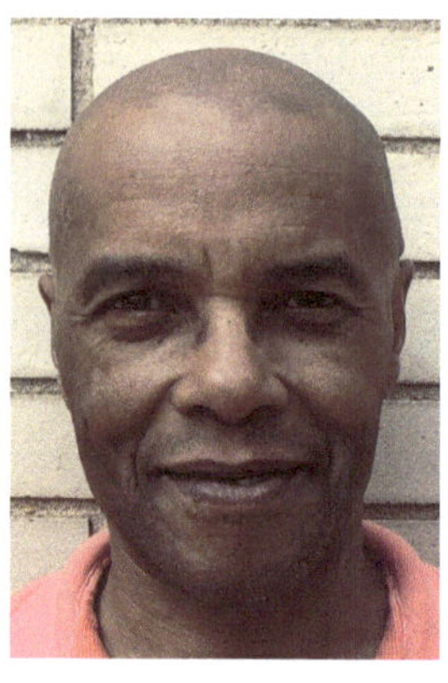

Carlton Lewis Sampson

Carlton Lewis Sampson, a poet and graphic novel author, has produced three other publications in collaboration with three different artists. *The Jerusalem 14, ...heresy of the highest accord* is a tale of the love between Mary Magdalene and Jesus of Nazareth, illustrated by Alexander T. Lee. *Po Lyn Lee; Ophelia House* is a horror fiction fantasy about belief and social class, illustrated by Andrew L. Willis. *Phascist Clowns; D.I.T.O. Live!*, a political fiction fantasy warning of consolidated wealth, is illustrated by Chris Robinson. Carlton Lewis Sampson's books are available online at carltonlewissampson.com and amazon.com.

The Jerusalem 14, ...heresy of the highest accord

Jesus of Nazareth was consumed by their passion but Mary Magdalene owed the moneychangers a personal debt. Seducing Jesus was necessary, easier for Mary than not falling in love. Deceived by Mary and betrayed by his newfound Zealot friends, Jesus realizes his destiny is part of a greater plan. Illustrated by Alexander T. Lee, *The Jerusalem 14, ...heresy of the highest accord,* is a tale of the love between Mary Magdalene and Jesus of Nazareth. This 48-page black and white illustrated poetic narrative is available online at thejerusalem14.com and amazon.com.

Po Lyn Lee; Ophelia House

When Grandmother, majesty of a secret sisterhood, sends Po, her trained she demon, a message to assassinate the president of the United States, Po's incidental romantic encounter with an artist leads Po to question Grandmother's messages and reject her conditioned demonic behavior. Po, a cannibal, realizing she is a demon, struggles with self-awareness, self-discovery, and humanity amidst the glamour, intrigue, espionage and morality of the global elite. Illustrated by Andrew L. Willis, *Po Lyn Lee; Ophelia House*, is a horror fiction fantasy about belief and social class. This 574-page, full color, graphic novel was published as 12 single-chapter issue comic book series and as a collected volume, available online at polynlee.com and amazon.com.

Phascist Clowns; D.I.T.O. Live!

The Phascist Clowns are the members of the Circus, descendants of interconnected families controlling the key natural resources and organizations with the majority of influence over the billions of socialites (people) living on the planet Socia. When Circus member Heir Head, global leader of industry, visits one of his top-secret munitions facilities to witness the testing of a new weapon system, he encounters mayhem and terrorism, symptoms of the social extremes caused by the Circus. Illustrated by Chris Robinson, *Phascist Clowns; D.I.T.O. Live!* is a political fiction fantasy, warning of consolidated wealth. This 28-page black and white comic book is available online at phascistclowns.com and amazon.com.

About the Artist

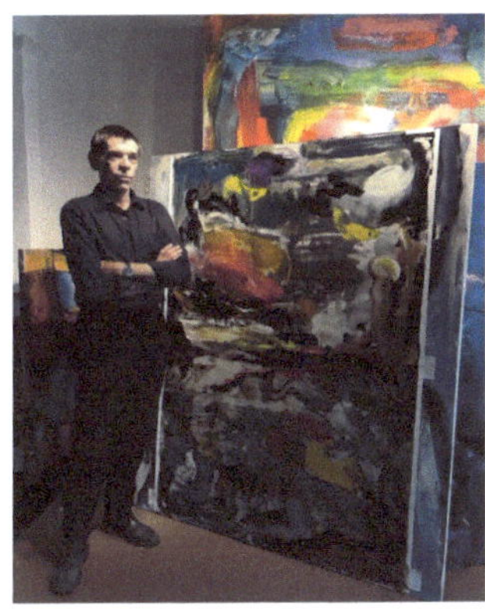

Alfred Ortega

Born in Philadelphia, Alfred Ortega studied painting and sculpture at the Pennsylvania Academy of the Fine Arts. Ortega's work is currently represented by the Atlantic Gallery, Nantucket and the Ligne Roset Gallery, New York. Ortega has exhibited at the Woodmere Museum and Twenty-two Gallery in Philadelphia. The artist's work is represented in the permanent collection of the Pennsylvania State Museum and in private collections.

Noted for his bold use of color, Ortega's paintings and oil prints emanate primal energy. His prominent, large canvases reveal a dynamic world populated with vibrant forms and figures barely contained within their frames. A master monoprint maker, Ortega's vivid oil prints of figures, landscapes, and portraits are animated by an unabashed freedom of form and color and a daring love of life.

To view the complete portfolio of Alfred Ortega's work, please visit alfredortega.com.

For more information about the paintings, contact Alfred Ortega at alfredortega@me.com.

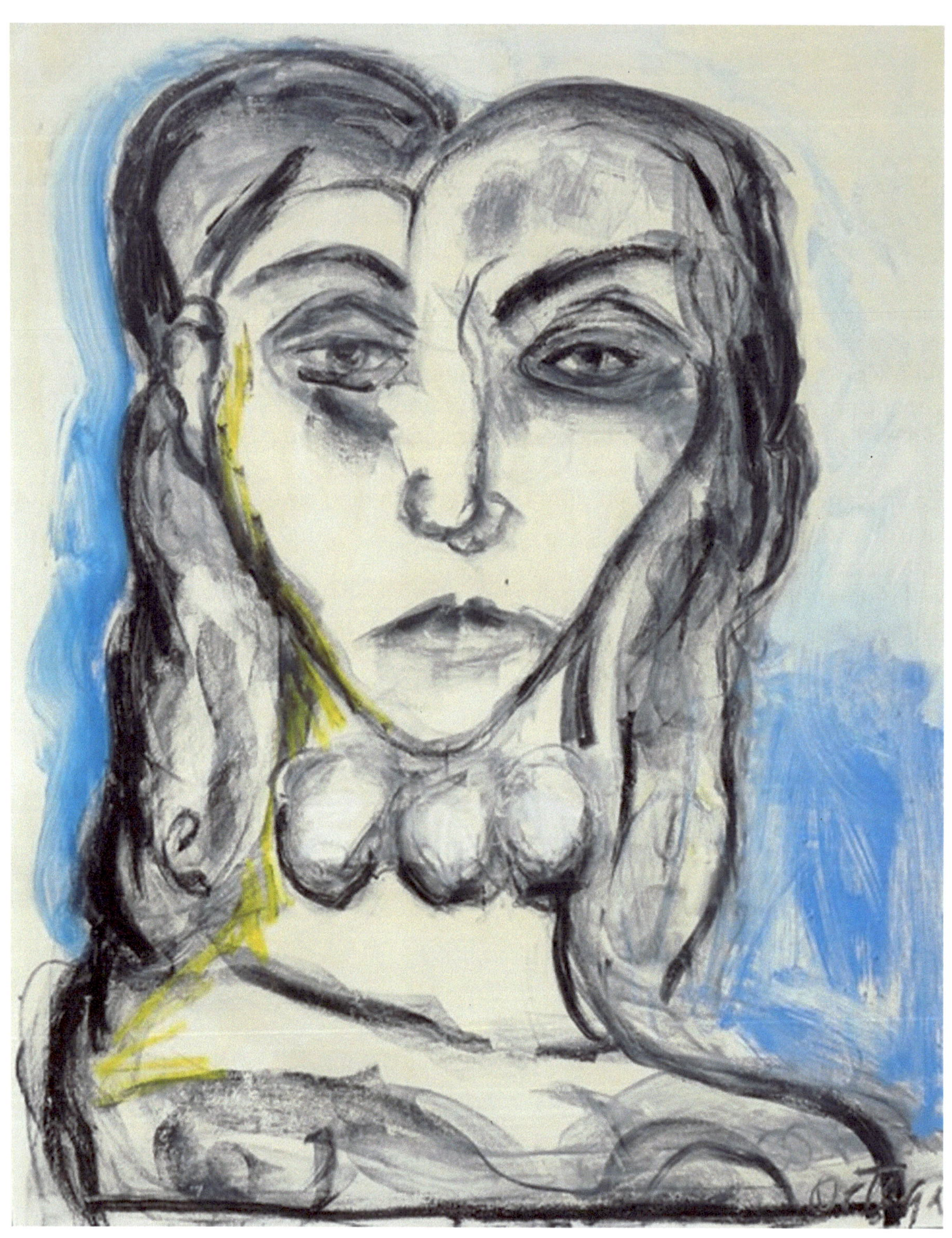

Portrait of a Young Girl

www.ingramcontent.com/pod-product-compliance
Lightning Source LLC
LaVergne TN
LVHW070151110826
845147LV00002B/370

* 9 7 8 1 9 5 3 1 3 2 0 1 7 *